A Brief Introduction to Kemetian
By Faheem J

A BRIEF INTRODU(
COSMOLOGY, SIGNS, SYMBOLS, AND RITUALS

BY FAHEEM JUDAH-EL D.D. D.M.

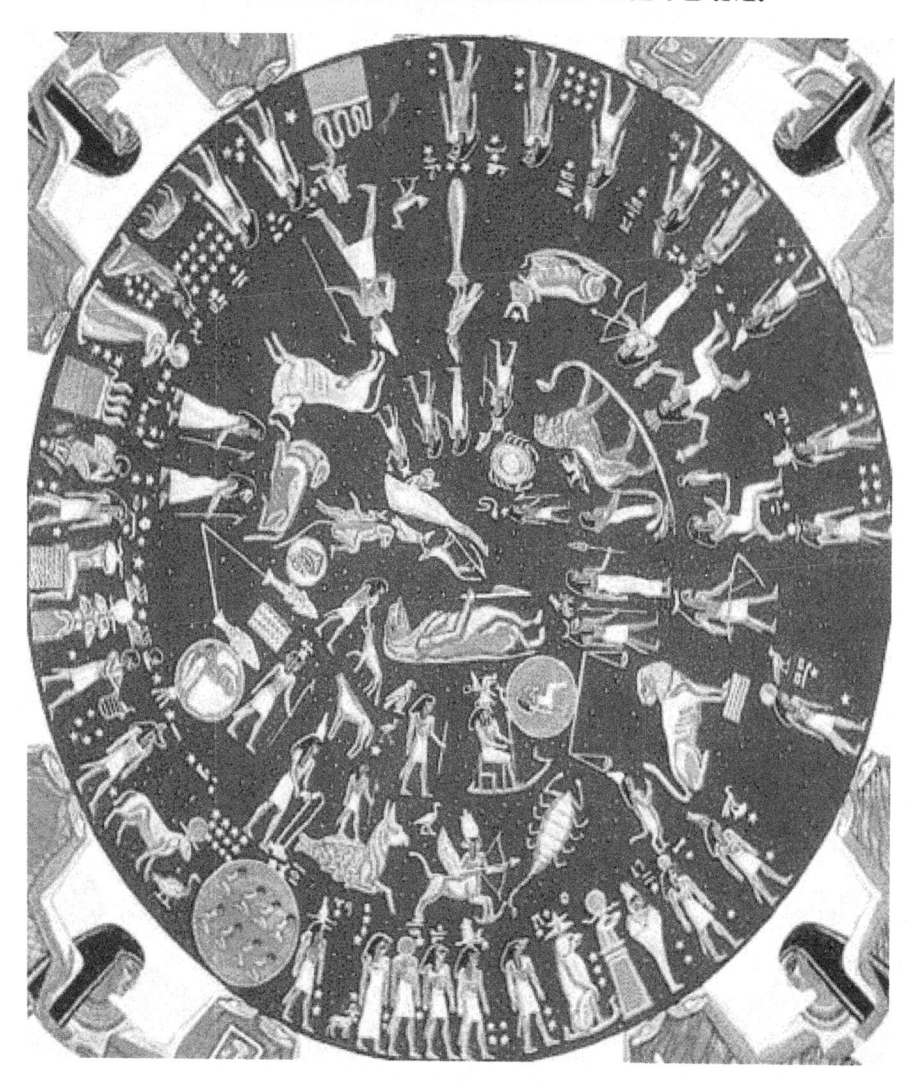

Published by Rising Sun Publications 2020 ©

A BRIEF INTRODUCTION TO KEMETIAN COSMOLOGY, SIGNS, SYMBOLS, AND RITUALS

BY FAHEEM JUDAH-EL D.D. D.M.

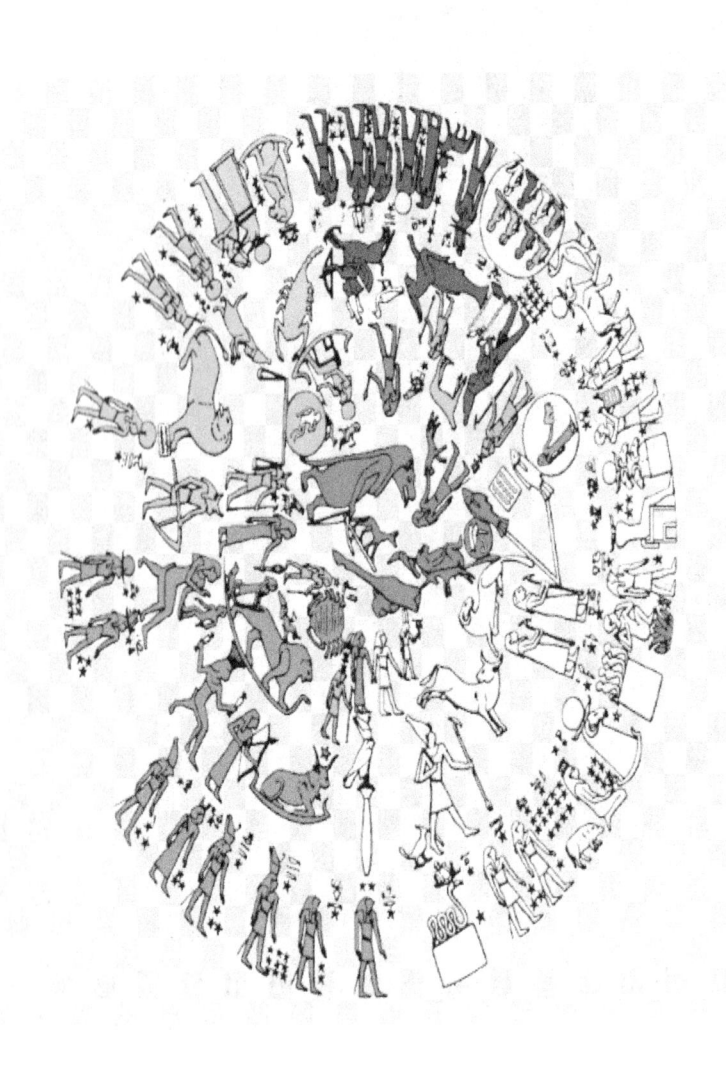

Table of Contents

About the Author	P.4
Part One Introduction	P.5
The work of Gerald Massey	P.17
Seasonal Significance	P.21
Part Two Resurrection	P.24
Heru-Horus Scopes the universal attributes in man	P.36
Those born under the sign of Tehuti	P.49
Those born under the sign of Heru (Horus)	P.50
Those born under the sign of Amun (Amen)	P.69
Those born under the sign of Anbu (Anubis)	P.72
Those born under the sign of Set (Seth)	P.74
Those born under the sign of Mut (Moot)	P.80
Those born under the sign of Shu (Shoo)	P.82
Those born under the sign of Geb	P.84
Those born under the sign of Het Heru	P.86
Those born under the sign of Auset (Isis)	P.88
The pre-creative state of the world and cosmology	
Questions and Answers	P.92

ABOUT THE AUTHOR

Faheem Judah-EL was born September 15th, 1962 in Decatur Illinois. He is considered one of America's most prominent Meta-physicians or Spiritual Scientists. Faheem has studied many spiritual disciplines such as The Egyptian Mysteries - The Greater Mysteries, Christianity-The Lesser Mysteries, The Ethiopian Mysteries, Metaphysics, Sumerian Theology, The Dogon Mystery Traditions, Sufi Traditions, Kundalini Chakra System, and the Allegorical Life of Christ. He has written and published many books on spiritual concepts. Mr. Judah-EL has traveled to many parts of the world such as Ethiopia, Egypt, Mecca, Mexico, Kenya, South Africa, Uganda, and many Native American Mound Centers of North America. Currently, Mr. Judah-EL is an author, editor, and publisher at Axum Publication.

PART ONE
INTRODUCTION

This book takes a brief look at the concepts of Ancient Kemetian cosmology from a modern point of view. We will also look at Kemetian symbols and meanings in the stars as they apply to the personality and attributes of modern man. Kemetian cosmology is not abstract, it is not devil worship, and it is not contrary to practices written about in biblical texts or other sacred scriptures. It is humanistic, logical, analytical, and rational. The reader will discover the Kemetian concept of MAN IS THE UNIVERSE, AND THE UNIVERSE IS MAN. Kemetians along the African Nile Valley did not believe in religion as people do today, they were in-tune with ALL, in nature, and one with the cosmos. Modern-day religions are but remnants of these great universal principles.

Kemetian temples and social and political structures were also a reflection of the universe, which interacted between the nine universal realms. This book gives a brief background of the Kemetian centers of cosmological knowledge such as Denerah temple complex, and the rituals that connected heaven to earth, and served as a gateway for resurrection and new life.

In the west, it is taught that the Greeks were the first to chart the stars and to understand the cosmic effect of the stars on the destiny of people born within specific dates groups, but this is not true, long before the Greeks charted the stars the Ancient Kemetians of the African Nile Valley had charted the stars and had advance knowledge of star's names and positions and their effects on human beings and the earth.

(Note* Cosmological centers such as Ta-Apet, or Khmunu may varying concepts on cycles times and dates in various mythos but not scientific facts)

The widely accepted knowledge about cosmology, spirituality, architecture and other Kemetian sciences come to us from the interpretations of western academia from the Kemetian texts.

Their interpretations are restricted by their western and Judeo-Christian concepts, totally ignoring the people, customs, and traditions of modern people whose way of life have not changed for over 3000 years, I am speaking of the Oromo, Afars, Medjay, and many tribes of Ethiopia, Sudan and Eritrea.

Most of western academia solely rely on Greek and Roman interpretations, and ignore the eyewitness accounts of ancient historians such as Herodotus, Plutarch, Plat, Diodorus, and others who witness the advanced culture of the original Kemetians of the African Nile Valley in their golden age.

THE ONE IS ALL, AND ALL IS ONE

THE NETERU –*NETJERU – NETCHERU*

The Ancient Kemetians of the African Nile Valley knew of the One Creature who was self-produced, self-existent, immortal, invisible, eternal, omniscient, and almighty. This Creator was represented through the functions and attributes in nature and in the universe. These attributes were known as the Neteru – Netjeru (pronounced Net-jer-u; masculine singular; Netjer, feminine singular: Netjert). The modern terms god and goddesses are a mistranslation of the Kemetian term Netjeru.

Dendera Temple complex of the African Nile Valley
Built beginning ca. 1995 BCE

Full front view of Het Heru Temple

The temple complex at Dendera is quite large, boasting a basilica, two birth houses, a sacred lake, and numerous other temples and shrines within its walls. Structures at the site hail from an assortment of different ancient Kemetian eras.

A Brief Introduction to Kemetian Cosmology, Signs, Symbols, and Rituals
By Faheem Judah-El D.D. D.M.

Main Hall front view of Het Heru Temple

There is evidence that the first building on the site went up around 2250 BCE.

In 1995 BCE, construction likely began on the Mentuhotep II monument, the oldest existing structure when the site was rediscovered. The Mentuhotep monument has since been moved to Cairo.

Painted sandstone seated statue of Nebhepetre Mentuhotep II

The oldest structure currently there is from Nectanebo II, built ca. 345 BCE. The structure may have begun in 54 BCE, when construction began on the Temple of HetHeru, the most prominent structure at the Dendera complex.

NST BTY – PHAROAH NECTANEBO

The nose removed to hide Nisu Bity Nectanebo's African Identity

Dendera complex

The Temple of Het Heru is one of the most well-preserved antiquity sites of ancient Kemet today, and is an excellent example of traditional Nisu-Pharaonic architecture. The Temple of Het-Heru was built primarily as a cosmological center and to give reverence to the Netjert Het Heru.

In the Kemetian Mystery at Dendera during a period known as the **Happy Reunion**, Het-Heru would journey from her temple to spend some time with her husband, Heru, at his temple in Edfu. This **"reunion"** was a yearly occurrence, and at the end of the celebration, the return of Het-Heru to Dendera was thought to signal the official beginning of the inundation season of the Nile.

A Brief Introduction to Kemetian Cosmology, Signs, Symbols, and Rituals
By Faheem Judah-El D.D. D.M.

The sacred lake at Dendera

Side view of the birthing Temple of Het-Heru at Dendera

The temple of Het-Heru originally housed the famous **Zodiac of Dendera**. This bas-relief with human and animal figures represented a night sky cape, and was found on the ceiling of a chapel in the Temple of Het-Heru, where the mysteries of the resurrection of the Netjer Ausar were celebrated. Western educators determined it should be interpreted as a map of the sky only rather than a giant horoscope (horus scope) or a perpetual astrological tool. **(An area out of their expertise)**

The particular configuration of the planets among the constellations shown in the Zodiac of Dendera occurs only about once every thousand years. Two astrophysicists have dated it between June 15 and August 15, 50 BCE. Two eclipses are represented on the Zodiac exactly where they occurred at that time.

A Brief Introduction to Kemetian Cosmology, Signs, Symbols, and Rituals
By Faheem Judah-El D.D. D.M.

The veiling of Aset   (Life Magazine)

Question: is the Dendera Zodiac the only Egyptian map of the heavens?

Answer: The Dendera Zodiac is the only circular depiction of astronomy to be found within Kemetian antiquity. All other references to the zodiac or astrology are either square or pyramidal in shape and design. The zodiac itself depicts the 360 days of the Kemetian year, with thirty-six decans arranged in a circular fashion.

Question: what is a Decan?

Answer: A decan represents one-third of the duration of a zodiacal constellation. Twelve signs with three decans each means thirty-six decans in total. This is a metric measurement that western astrologers continue to use to this day.

Zodiac Ceiling in the Temple of Het-Heru

THE WORK OF GERALD MASSEY

Renowned English Egyptologist/Researcher Gerald Massey reconciled each of the traditional western zodiacal signs with a Kemetian counterpart after more than twenty years of research.

Looking at the **Dendera Zodiac**, the ram of **Aries** corresponds with the ram-headed deity *Amun.* **Taurus** corresponds with **Ausar**, sometimes referred to as **"The Bull of Eternity",** while the two fish of **Pisces** is signified by two crocodiles swimming in opposite directions. For every constellation in the traditional western zodiac there is a Kemetian equivalent with the same symbolism; ranging from *Khnum* the goat with the same characteristics as **Capricorn,** to **Atum**, the lion-headed deity that bears resemblance to **Leo**. The image of **Auset** carrying **Heru** in her arms is synonymous with the constellation of **Virgo,** and bears resemblance to the image of the **Virgin Mary** carrying **Jesus**. Clearly the ancient Kemetian Dendera Zodiac of the African Nile Valley was the original, copied by Greeks and later cultures.

www.lulu.com/spotlight/egipt

A Brief Introduction to Kemetian Cosmology, Signs, Symbols, and Rituals
By Faheem Judah-El D.D. D.M.

The figures represented in the Dendera Zodiac correspond to the traditional zodiacal signs

A Brief Introduction to Kemetian Cosmology, Signs, Symbols, and Rituals
By Faheem Judah-El D.D. D.M.

The figures represented in the traditional zodiacal signs correspond to the Dendera Zodiac.

Seasonal Significance

Question: What were these symbols meant to convey, and what importance did the Ancient Egyptians place on them?
Answer: For the Kemetians, each zodiac sign corresponded with a season of the year that was believed to be ruled over by a specific Netjer (Deity).
Question: can you give us an example?
Answer: Khepri-Ra, the scarab beetle signifying Cancer was symbolic of summer, while **Maat,** the scales of Libra signified the autumnal equinox.
Question: all of the symbols are not directly in a circular pattern do we know why?
Answer: great question, very observant, and the answer is no, we don't know exactly why. All twelve of the constellations appear in the Dendera Zodiac, but the placements of some are somewhat distorted. Let's look at the crab of Cancer; it seems to have been deliberately placed towards the center of the zodiac, resulting in a spiral-like configuration of the zodiac. It is uncertain why it was designed that way; the Cancer month may have held a particular significance.

To the Kemetians of the African Nile Valley, each season had a unique effect on the passing of days within the 360-day calendar. The hours in a day were not measured in a static and fixed fashion, but were subject to change from season to season. The zodiac also depicted the movement of the star **Septu - Sirius;** a very important star to the Ancient Kemetians as you will see later on in this book. Sirius rising from the horizon marked the beginning of the New Year; however this date would change by eight and a half days every thousand years. The sign of Aquarius was given great importance, as it represented the sign of inundation, signifying a time of flood. The Ancient Kemetians would use Sirius as a marker to indicate when the annual flooding of the Nile would occur, in what we would now call the month of June.

Asar's Belt

The representations of the signs of the Greek zodiac as we know them today did not appear in ancient Kemet until the Greco-Roman Period. During that period the original knowledge of the signs, symbols, and mysteries of the Zodiac of Dendera couldn't be interpreted correctly by western academia. Only a few Nebs (Masters) knew the true meanings of the symbolism.

As time passed foreign cultural elements merged with post-Kemetian culture such as Babylonian and Greek astronomical and astrological theories, and as a result of the Assyrian and Babylonian deportations of the eighth and sixth centuries BCE, and the Persian and Greek invasions of the sixth and fourth centuries BCE the true knowledge of the Dendera Zodiac was lost forever to those un-initiated in the Greater Mysteries.

Question: where is the Dendera Zodiac today?

Answer: the Zodiac of Dendera was transported to France in 1821, with the permission of Mohamed Ali Pasha, who was the Turkish viceroy of Modern Egypt at the time. The modern Egyptian government has asked for its return. It currently is on display at the Louvre in Paris.

Main Entrance of the Sun in the Temple of Het-Heru

A Brief Introduction to Kemetian Cosmology, Signs, Symbols, and Rituals
By Faheem Judah-El D.D. D.M.

PART TWO
RESURRECTION

Septu – Sirius Star Complex

Aun Ra the Opening of the Mouth

Ausar's belt known as Orion's belt

A Brief Introduction to Kemetian Cosmology, Signs, Symbols, and Rituals
By Faheem Judah-El D.D. D.M.

The astronomical Three Kings

Question: What was the Egyptian concept of heaven called?

Answer: In ancient Kemetian mythology, the fields of Aaru (Ancient **Kemetian**: "Reeds, rushes"), known also as the Field of Reeds, is the heavenly paradise where Ausar rules once he had displaced Anbu in the Ogdoad. ... It was the KA of the Nile Delta.

Question: what is the significance of Orion's belt or the Sirius constellation?

Answer: Resurrection.

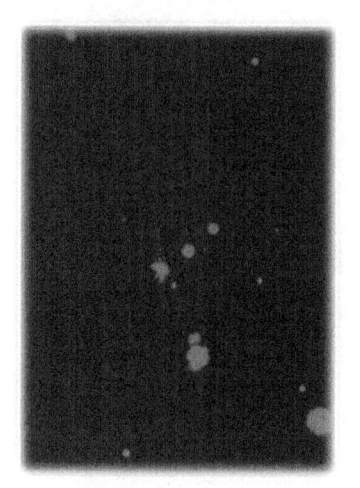

Sirius And Orion   **The Orion Constellation**

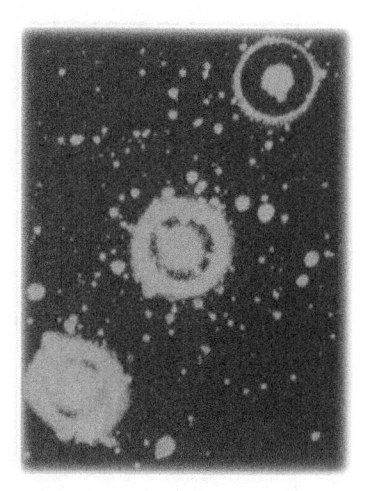

PA SAHU

Question: In one of your books you mentioned Pa Sahu, can you explain what it is?

Answer: Pa Sahu: refers to *"The Orion"* constellation which is a constellation in the celestial equator near Gemini and Taurus, containing the stars Betelgeuse and Rigel, of middle English **Orioun**, from Latin (Oriōn), from the Greek **Ouranos** meaning "heaven *or haven*", a "docking point". To the ancient Kemetians **Sahu** *"Orion"* was the most important star in the sky. The ancient Kemetian's Sothic calendar consisted of 365 ¼ days, which is a cycle consisting of 1,460 years of 365 days in the Ancient Kemetian calendar, the apparent calendar. Then the ancient Kemetian's mystic brotherhood called **The Ancient Kemetian Order** had the mystery calendar based on **the sacred composite number 19**, in the apparent calendar.

The opening of the mouth ceremony

Question: When did the "Opening of the Mouth Ceremony" take place?

Answer: The opening of the mouth ceremony took place at the first appearance of **Sahu** *"Orion"* on the eastern horizon just before the sun travels from the **Duat** *"underworld"* after 70 days. This was called the heliacal rising of **Pa Sebt** *"The Sirius"*, the Dog Star symbol of **Anbu** *"Anubis"*, whose symbol is the black dog wearing the red necklace (scarf), cynocephalus.

The dog was a symbol of the guide, being it was the jackal that helped Auset locate the grave of Ausar (Osiris), and thus the dog star and its movement in the equinox points out the great secret of the renewal of our story every 25,000 years. The heliacal rising is seen as **Sahu** *"Ausar-Orion"* and the sun joined together at the moment.

ANUBIS WITH RED SCARF

Ra Travelling On His Solar Ark, Crescent Boat

From The Duat (Underworld)

Question: When did this event take place?

Answer: The event occurred once a year and gave rise to the Sothic or Sothis, the star **Sept** "*Sirius*" calendar the constellation of Canis Major, the brightest star in the sky, 8.1 light – years distant from Ta (Earth). Sothis is Latin (Sirius), from the Greek Seirios, from Seirios, meaning burning.

The blazing star, the bright star in the sky, is the symbol of **Aset** "*Isis*"

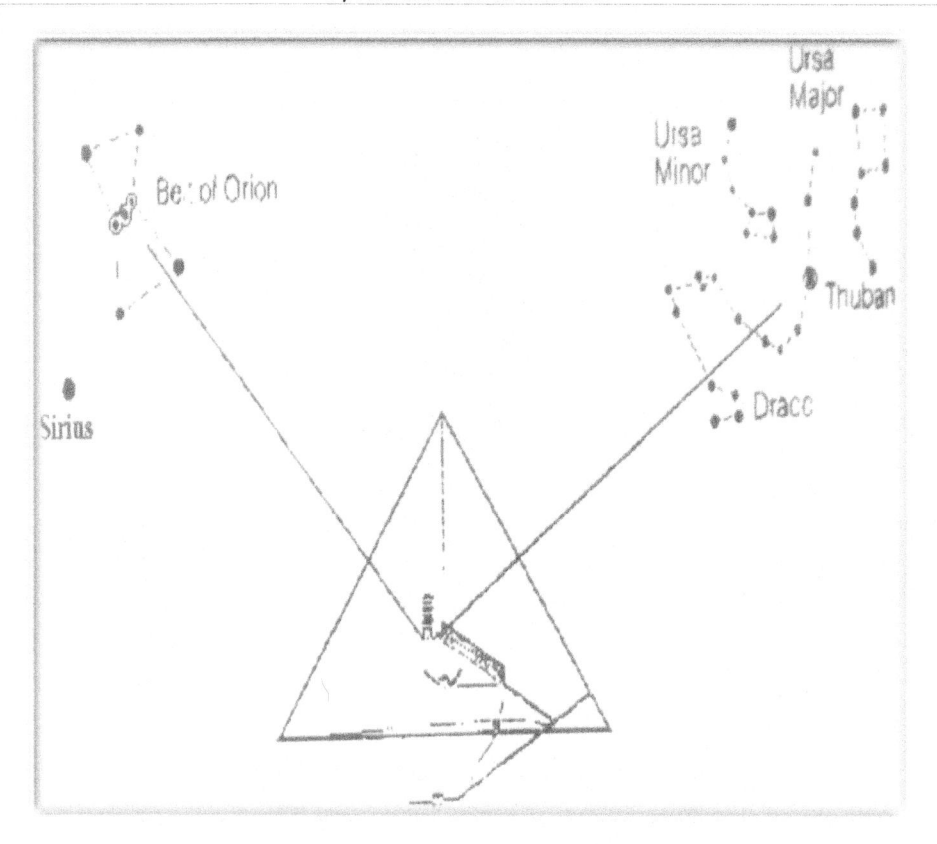

A Brief Introduction to Kemetian Cosmology, Signs, Symbols, and Rituals
By Faheem Judah-El D.D. D.M.

The Heliacal Rising of the Orion Constellation

Question: This must have been very important to the Egyptians am I right?

Answer: The heliacal rising of **Sahu** "*Orion*" was so important to the ancient Kemetians that gigantic temples were constructed with their main aisles **"passageways"**, oriented precisely towards the spot on the horizon where **Sahu** "*Orion*" would appear on the expected daylight hours. One such temple to the star **Sahu** "*Orion*" was the temple of **Auset** "*Isis*" which sat on the high terrace at the south end of the temple of (HetHeru) **Hat – Har**, "*Hathor*", protected by the Neter **Bes**. It's in the city of Denderah at **Waret** "*luxor*" in Nubia.

A Brief Introduction to Kemetian Cosmology, Signs, Symbols, and Rituals
By Faheem Judah-El D.D. D.M.

Statue of Bes

**Hathor's Temple at Denderah, Luxor
Kemet In North East Africa**

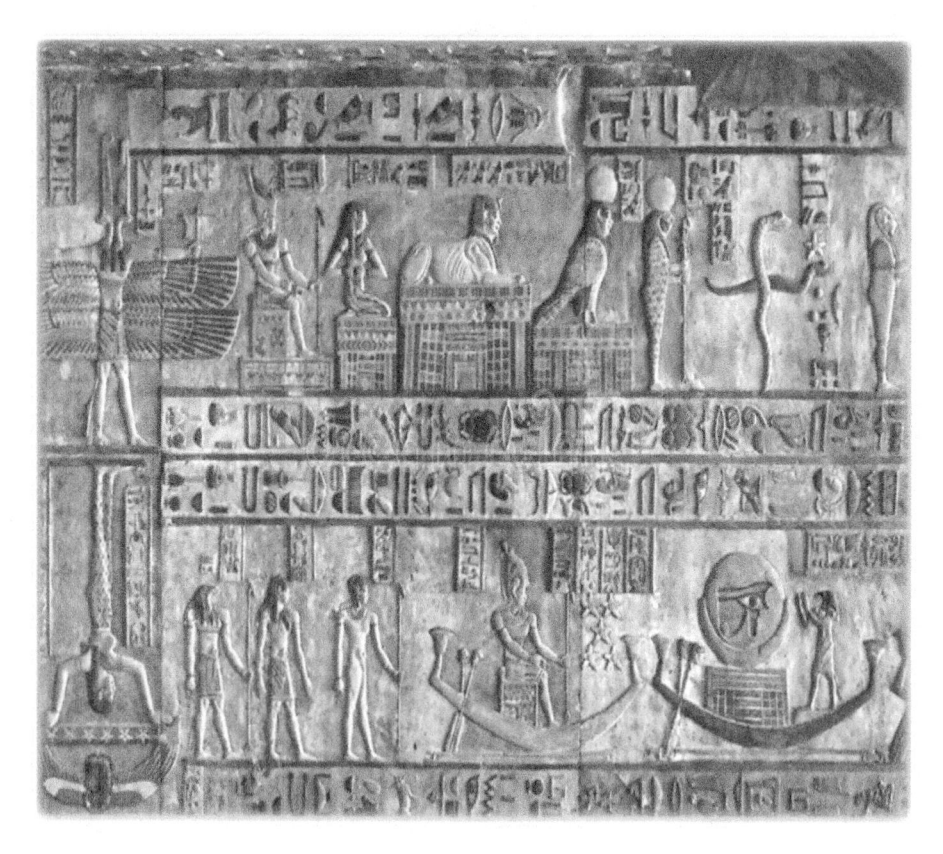

Hathor's Temple at Denderah, Luxor

Kemet in North East Africa

Question: What is the "opening of the mouth" ritual take place, and how did it take place?

Answer: When A Nisu bity - Pharaoh passed away, he was mummified then encased in an outer shell. The opening of The Mouth Ceremony was one of the great ascension rituals in the African Nile Valley.

The Nisu-Pharaoh's consort and his still mortal son or sons must cause new life to stir in him at the exact moment of the early Rising of Orion; the Pharaoh must be reborn, or resurrected. (See the book Aun-Ra)

The Opening of the Mouth Ceremony

An Astral View of Heru Performing The

Opening Of the Mouth Ceremony, Below Are His Four Sons

While He Is Waiting To Have His/Her Mouth Opening Ceremony (**Mishfut**) A New Life Resurrection, He Is Referred To As A **Khon** "Dead" Awaiting His Fourth Resurrection Having Been Buried Three Times Before.

Anubis preparing the "Khon" deceased to be raised to new life
This is known as Krst – Christ – anointing the body

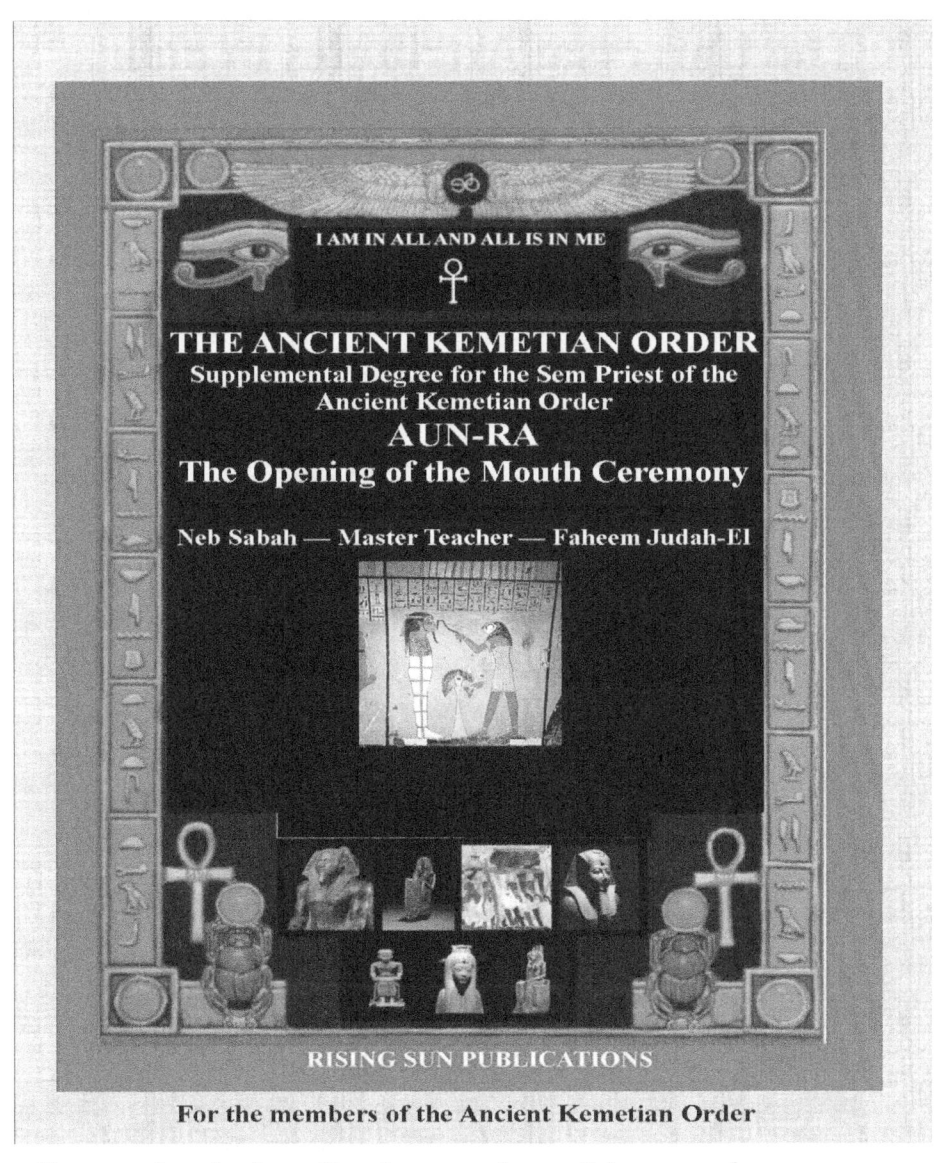

See my book Aun-Ra the opening of the mouth ceremony
www.lulu.com/spotlight/egipt

A Brief Introduction to Kemetian Cosmology, Signs, Symbols, and Rituals
By Faheem Judah-El D.D. D.M.

HERU – HORUS-SCOPE
The Universal Attributes in man

A Brief Introduction to Kemetian Cosmology, Signs, Symbols, and Rituals
By Faheem Judah-El D.D. D.M.

Kemetian zodiac sign:	Corresponding Greek-western zodiac sign:
Osiris - Ausar	Aries personality
Amun-Ra	Taurus personality
Seth - Sutuwk	Gemini personality
Bastet - Bas	Cancer personality
Anubis - Anbu	Leo personality
Thoth – Tehuti (Djehuti)	Virgo personality
Geb, Keb	Libra personality
Mut	Scorpio personality
Hapi	Sagittarius personality
Heru	Capricorn personality
Sekhmet	Aquarius personality
Isis - Auset	Pisces personality

THOTH, TEHUTI, DJEHUTI

A Brief Introduction to Kemetian Cosmology, Signs, Symbols, and Rituals
By Faheem Judah-El D.D. D.M.

Kemetian - April 1-19 and November 8-17

Attributes: Wise, creative, Intelligent, one of action

Question: What does Tehuti's name mean?

Answer: The meaning of Tehuti's name ("Dhwtii" or "Djehuti"), represented on the Medu Neter as the Ibis, is unknown. Western academia thinks his name may mean "he of Djehout" (an unknown place or realm), "he of the house of speech", "he who speaks in the temple", or "messenger", "he who selects", or "he who chooses" but these are only conjecture.

Some scientists believe that "DHw" could have been the oldest name of the Ibis bird, implying that Tehuti would mean: "he who has the nature of the Ibis". Tehuti holds many attributes, or an accumulation of *cognitive* divinities.

Question: How was the Ibis depicted?

Answer: The Ibis bird appeared perched on a slate of palettes in the Terminal Pre-dynastic Period. The sacred Ibis had a long curved beak, suggestive of the crescent New Moon, and black & white feathering reminiscent of the lunar phases of waxing & waning.

The sacred Ibis bird of the African Nile Valley

A Brief Introduction to Kemetian Cosmology, Signs, Symbols, and Rituals
By Faheem Judah-El D.D. D.M.

Tehuti the Sacred Neter of Wisdom, Scribe of Ra

In the Old Kingdom, the association between the Ibis and Tehuti already existed, so in the afterlife, the wings of Tehuti carried the Nisu (Pharaoh) over the celestial river.

*Note Nisu – NSU means Emperor – King

*Note Neter – NTR means divinities in nature, natural, nurture

According to one Kemetian legend, Tehuti's birth was unnatural (he sprang from the Neter Seth's head). Tehuti was known as the tongue of Ra, the messenger of Ra, and the **"Scribe of the Neteru"**. It was Tehuti who promulgated Atum-Re's laws.

Atum-Re

Tehuti was the great unifier among the divinities, because the **"peace of the Neteru"** is in him. He was a traveler and an international divinity, for his name can be found in many ancient languages such as: Babylonian, Coptic, Aramaic, Ge'ez, Greek & Latin. Tehuti was the Neter of all knowledge and literature. He invented writing, a scribe himself; he was the overseer of all the divine books in the House of Life held in all major temples of ancient Kemet. The great wisdom of Tehuti was highly revered and considered too sacred for common eyes to see.

Tehuti was known as the "son of Ra" and "Lord of the eight Neteru" (the Ogdoad of Hermopolis).

*Note - the word Ogdoad means eight

* Note – Hermopolis means the city of Hermes (Roman for Tehuti)

In the funerary rituals, Tehuti acted the part of the recorder of the judgment of the deceased soul: he observed whether the heart (mind) of the deceased was as light as the feather of Maat, or light enough to balance the feather of truth & justice. His original home was **Khemenu, or "eight-town"**, referring to the four pairs of mythical Neteru of chaos **(scientific for primordial waters, infinity of space, darkness, and invisibility)** which existed before creation, of which Tehuti became the Master, he was known as the **Master of the city of eight.** The Greeks called it Hermopolis ("city of Hermes").

Question: Can you explain a little of the Hermopolitan Theology?

Answer: In Hermopolitan **(Khemenu)** theology the Nun **(place of all potential)** was personified by the Ogdoad (city of eight), showing that this theology was intimately linked with the **"mind of Re"** speaking its Great Word (the sacred Ibis dropping the Great Word in the limitless ocean of inert possibilities known as the Nun), which transformed the pre-creational, chaotic Ogdoad (cf. the four female snake-divinities & the four male frog-divinities) into the Ennead of Hermopolis **(Supreme Nine of Khemenu)** headed by the "first of the eight", the Great Word of Re. The Hermopolitan scheme is mental-cognitive, conceptual and promotes the Kemetian concept that speech has creative & magical power-Heka, transforming powers.

*Note (This was all pre-dynastic)

The Ogdaod or the four pairs, symbolic of duality

As in Memphite theology (Men-Nefer) of Ptah, the original great Neter (Tehuti) creates it all with divine words in his mind and on his tongue. (Later adapted into Greek logos-Philosophy)

The Heliopolitan (Kemenu) concept added the self-generative aspect of the divinity, as well as the eternal participation (from the first moment) between the one (Atum) spitting out his children (Shu and Tefnut) and putting his arms around them to be as one again, or the first triad or trinity.

(This is where we get the phrase "a spitting image" of a child like its parent)

This is the first conceptualization of the Neter (Godhead) or a trinity of divine being expanding into millions) (Intra-divine multiplication.

Question: what does the attributes of Tehuti represent?

Answer: Tehuti represents the power of sound (the Word), as the prime mover of inert energy. Kemetian creation scrolls stress the knowledge of creation by the Word. In the Kemetian mythos it was the great Tehuti who uttered the words as directed by the great Neter Ra that created the world.

The Book of coming forth by day or Pert M Hru it reads: "I am the Eternal… I am that which created the Word…I am the Word…

Question: can you give us a sample of Tehuti as the representation of the power of sound?

Answer: Science tells us that around 15 billion years there was condensed energy in the place of all potential the Kemetians of the African Nile Valley called "The Nun". This is when the world was in a pre-creation state, the bible calls it the "Void".

Well this energy began to build up, until it finally exploded and expanded outward as a big explosion or big bang. This was the Word, or power of sound from the tongue of Tehuti, out of the mouth of Ra.

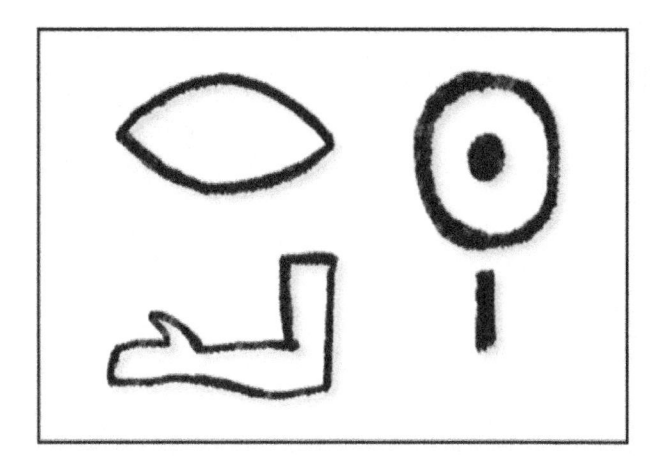

RA

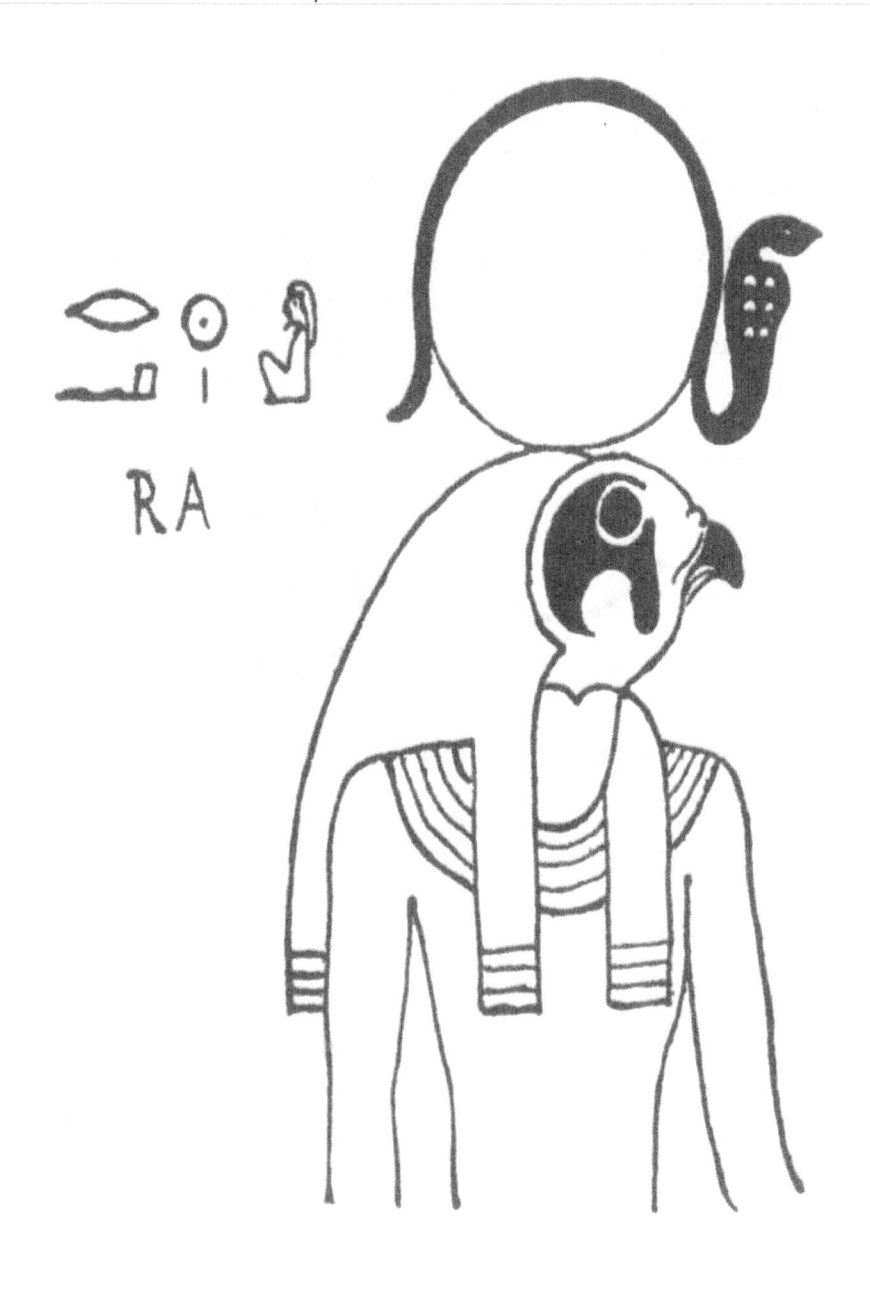

Metu Neter – RA Symbol

Question: so is Nun seen as good or evil?

Answer: Its' neither good nor evil it is states of pre-creative existence.

Question: what does that mean?

Answer: it means that out of "Nun" the place of all potential emerges creation, just as a baby comes out of the triple darkness of the womb of the mother. Nun is a chaotic state of existence where inert energy / matter is transformed into the parts of the universe as differentiated, orderly, structured, kinetic energies, in the form of thoughts, objects, and forces.

Question: is Tehuti known in other counties or cultures?

Answer: Yes as I have said before, Tehuti was known all over the ancient world by many cultures by many names. He was known as Hermes to the Greeks, Mercury to the Romans, and by many other names, but he was a sacred Neter in ancient Kemet known as the Master of the City of Eight (Ogdad) at Khmunu (Hermopolis), a Kemetian word meaning eight. (A symbol of pre-creation) His sacred day is Thursday, the day before Adam was created in Islam. Adam was created on Friday the day of Jumah.

(Note* on Thursday Sufis fast in recognition of Tehuti)

(Note* In Christianity Tehuti is equivalent to Gabriel/Michael)

(In Judaism Tehuti is associated with Enoch and Metatron)

Question: what is Tehuti's main divine attribute?

Answer: good question: Tehuti's has many but one of his main attributes is "action", the **Word** means action. In human terms we say "Word is bond" which means a man is only as good as his word. Tehuti represents the spoken and written word, language, recording the word, records, and knowledge and wisdom.

Question: was Tehuti portrayed only as an Ibis bird?

Answer: In Africa and most other indigenous peoples around the world associated nature with the elements and forces around them. Tehuti was portrayed as an Ibis headed male figure, or sometimes as a full ibis bird, Tehuti was also associated with the baboon, representing the spirit of dawn, the dawn of life in the creation process, coming out of Nun, or a pre-creative state.

Question: what does the Baboon represent?

Answer: Tehuti as the baboon represents ground zero of the cycle of the sun, or dawn in the morning, in Islam Fajr pray is made during ground zero or when the sun shows its first thread of light. The ancient Kemetians were fascinated with this point of beginning which represents a pre-creative state.

The Baboon – or Baba Moon, represents the point of beginning because the baboon is almost human, and it represents this crucial moment that precedes the awakening of the sun.

Question: does this a have a metaphysical meaning?

Answer: the Baboon represents this state in humans, just before they gain consciousness or awaken.

THOSE BORN UNDER THE SIGN OF TEHUTI

Tehuti-Djehuti is the Netjer of knowledge and wisdom. Those born under the sign of Tehuti are typically intelligent, listeners, accurate and capable problem-solvers, loyal in relationships, honest, great leaders, friendly, and observant. They are usually spiritual, analytical, and excellent organizers. Those born under the sign of Tehuti are researchers, recorders, patrons of women, decorators, planners, supervisors and managers, thrifty with money, but enjoy nice things in life.

Strengths: wise before their years, seasoned and original.

Weaknesses: rash, loner, head strong, impatient and self-rigorous.

Jobs assumed: authors - scribes, actors, lawyers and teachers.

Pa Neter Djehuty-Tehuti

A Brief Introduction to Kemetian Cosmology, Signs, Symbols, and Rituals
By Faheem Judah-El D.D. D.M.

Those born under the sign of Heru (Horus)

Kemetian - April 20 – May 7 and August 12-19

Based on Greek influence: September 28 – October 27

Pa Neter Heru

Question: Who is Heru?

Answer: Heru is the great Hawk, the spiritual man within, Heru means "He who is above", Heru is the origin of the Jesus Christ concept, Heru represents the divine principle realized.

Question: does Heru have any significance in human beings?

Answer: yes, Heru represents our soul journey, Heru represents overcoming of opposition (Set), and Heru is our example in life. **(Note* to be Heru-like, like in Christianity Christ-like)**

Question: In one of your books you talked about 3, 4, 5, as it pertains to Heru, can you explain it?

Answer: sure, and that is a good question, because as I have explained in many classes before, Heru is the offspring of the cosmic union between Auset (Isis) and Ausar (Osiris). The manifestation of Heru is also seen as the manifestation of the 3: 4: 5: Triangle.

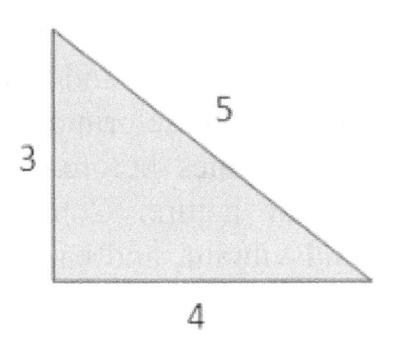

Question: what does that mean?

Answer: Any **triangle** whose sides are in the ratio **3:4:5** is a right **triangle**. Such **triangles** that have their sides in the ratio of whole numbers are called **Pythagorean Triples**. There are an infinite number of them, and this is just the smallest.

Question: can we find a source on this?

Answer: yes, read Plutarch in Moralia, Volume V. I will explain it to you in relationship to Heru. The number three (3) (Ausar/Osiris) is the first perfect odd number: four (4) is a square whose side is the even number two (2) (Auset/Isis); but five (Heru/Horus) is in some ways like his father, and in some ways like his mother, being made up of three (3) and two (2).

So when we look at the Pantheon of the Neteru we see that Panta – is a form of Penta which mean five (5). Five (5) is the perfect counting pattern, and Heru represents the number five (5) or Penta, which is the model for all Panta. (All Neteru)

Question: how did the ancient Egyptians come up with this idea?

Answer: well for the ancient Kemetians it wasn't just an idea the way people come up with ideas today, they overstood that everything in the universe is animated by life forces. Therefore, each particle is in constant movement and has interactions due to the effect of these life forces. These principles are called Neteru as I have explained many times before. Numbers designated these energetic aspects of nature. Consequently, the entire universe is animated and vibrant, and each facet is considered either "male" strong nuclear, or "female weak nuclear."

*(Hu Strong Nuclear, and Hee Weak Nuclear (HuHi)

Question: can you go a little deeper into 3, 4, 5, as it relates to ancient Kemet itself?

Answer: The concept of the relationships between 3, 4, and 5 is as ancient as old Kemet, and as old as the Great Pyramids themselves.

Question: do the pyramids hold secrets of this knowledge?

Answer: I can only tell you that those powerful, magnificent structures conceals deeply mystical knowledge that only recently have begun to be recognized by archeological research.

Question: do we have the knowledge today?

Answer: as far as 3, 4, 5, yes we know today exactly why the relationships between the numbers 3, 4, and 5 are so important, but it was a well-kept secret in ancient times.

Question: can you explain the Pythagorean Concept?

Answer: "Since the Pythagoreans considered the first ten numbers to be **seed patterns** for all the principles (Neteru) of the cosmos, a geometer needs only to create their shapes to model all the universal rhythms.

*Note the Grand Ennead or Supreme Nine and Ra (10)

The first three shapes to emerge from the vesica piscis, the triangle, square and pentagon (3, 4, 5) form the only relationship, or ratios, required to generate all the rest (except for seven). These relationships are called the square roots they are expressible not as whole numbers but as never-ending decimals. These ongoing relationships hold the structural pattern for all numbers and shapes that follow.

Question: can you talk about 3, 4, and 5, in relationship to the Great Pyramids?

Answer: I can tell you that the classical numbers 3, 4, 5 are represented in the very structure of the pyramid. The Great Pyramid of Giza was built in approximately 2560 BCE, at the time of the Old Kingdom: • "The number One is the whole structure itself. • The triangular faces represent the number 3, the square base is the number 4 and finally • the four corners plus its apex complete the number 5."

*Notes this also represents the elements: Ta Earth, MuWater, Nefu Air, Set Fire, and Hu Divine Utterance

The Kemetian Triangle is the constant relationships between the One – Neb-Er-Tcher, as the whole structure and 3-Ausar, 4-Auset, and 5- Heru as its indivisible components are clearly shown. These numbers had profound mystical symbolism that becomes explicit in the explanations related to the Pythagorean triangle.

Pyramid of Giza

Let's look at this illustration:

A Brief Introduction to Kemetian Cosmology, Signs, Symbols, and Rituals
By Faheem Judah-El D.D. D.M.

"The upright, may be likened to the male, the base to the female, and the hypotenuse to the child of both, and so Ausar [Osiris] may be regarded as the origin, Auset [Isis] as the recipient, and Heru [Horus] as the perfected result." The short side of the right angle triangle is named "Ausar," which corresponds to the Father. The longer side is "Auset," which corresponds to the Mother. And finally, the **hypotenuse** is called "Heru," which corresponds to the Son.

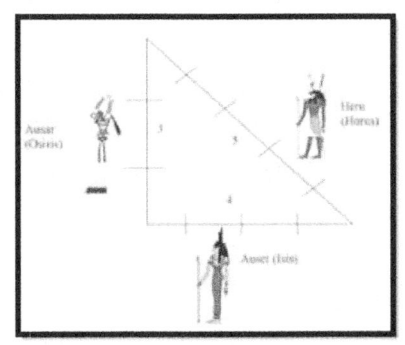

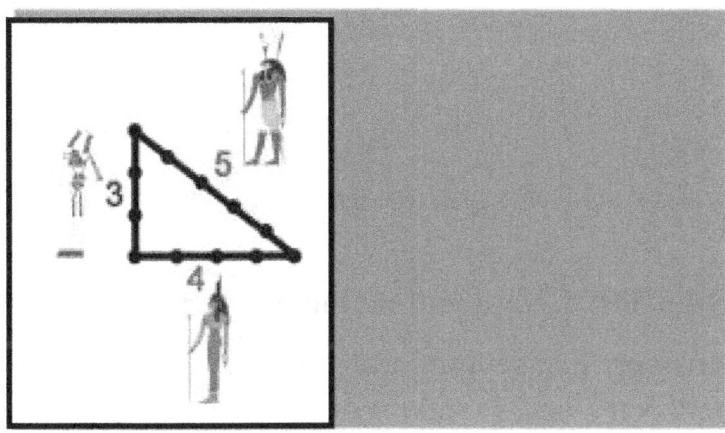

Pythagorean Triangle with Egyptian Attributions. Figures ©2007 by Jeff Dahl/Wikimedia Commons.

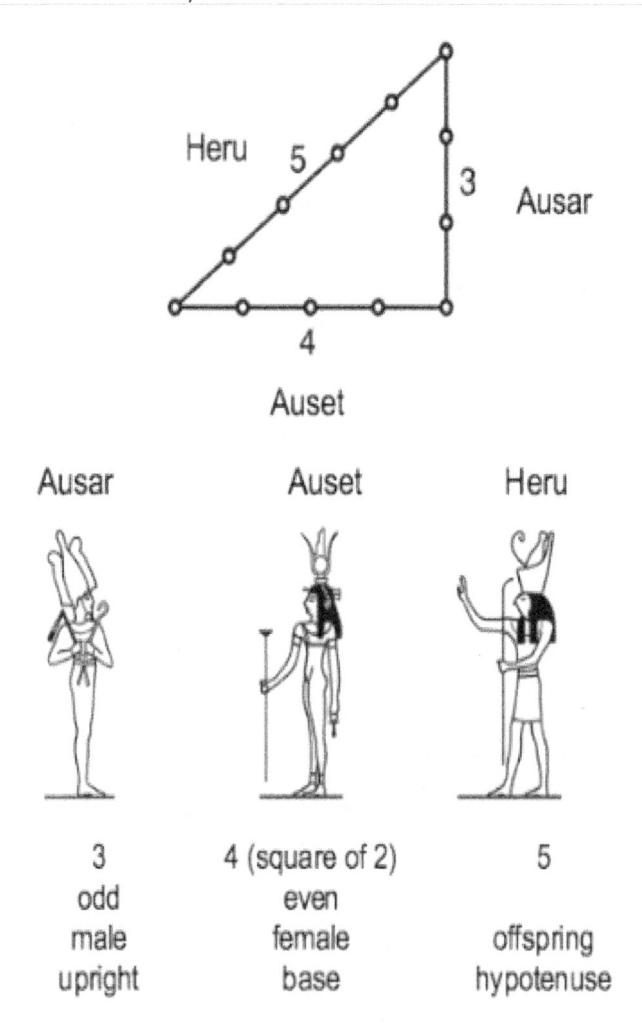

A Brief Introduction to Kemetian Cosmology, Signs, Symbols, and Rituals
By Faheem Judah-El D.D. D.M.

```
        Heru  5       3   Ausar
                  4
                Auset
```

Ausar	Auset	Heru
3	4 (square of 2)	5
odd	even	offspring
male	female	hypotenuse
upright	base	

Question: So are you saying numbers have attributes?

Answer: I'm saying look at the vitality and the interaction between 3 and 4 (square of 2), we can see that they are male and female, or active and passive, vertical and horizontal, so yes they do have energy and life within them.

Question: why are three the first perfect odd number and not one?

Answer: great question, because to the ancient Kemetians one was not an odd number.

Question: Why not?

Answer: because the number one was the essence of the underlying principle of numbers or it held both polarities positive and negative and all other numbers were made from the number one.

Question: so what does the number one represent?

Answer: it represents Unity, the Absolute as un-polarized energy. Islam teaches: "Allah is One, and has no partners". One is neither odd nor even, but both: because if added to an odd number, it makes it even, and vice-versa. So it combines the opposites odd and even, and all the other opposites in the universe. One or Unity (Al-Iklas) is a perfect, eternal, undifferentiated consciousness.

The Rhind Papyrus tells us:

"Rules for inquiring into nature and for knowing all that exists, every mystery, every secret"

Question: Can you explain the forms of Heru?

Answer: Heru is represented in several forms and aspects, the five most common forms of Heru that correspond with the stages of spiritualization are:

1. Heru Pa Khart – Heru the child

Question: What does his name mean?

Anwer: His name means Heru the Child. He is known as Harpocrates to the Greeks. This is known as the age of total dependency.

(*Note: This when the new spiritual self is totally dependent on the Soul (BA) represented as the nurturing mother)

Heru is shown as an infant child being suckled by his Holy mother Auset or Isis to the Greeks. Many cultures adopted this depiction of their Holy mother and child, which was later represented in Christianity as the Madonna and Child, and depiction of Mary and Jesus.

Ethiopian Orthodox Version

A Brief Introduction to Kemetian Cosmology, Signs, Symbols, and Rituals
By Faheem Judah-El D.D. D.M.

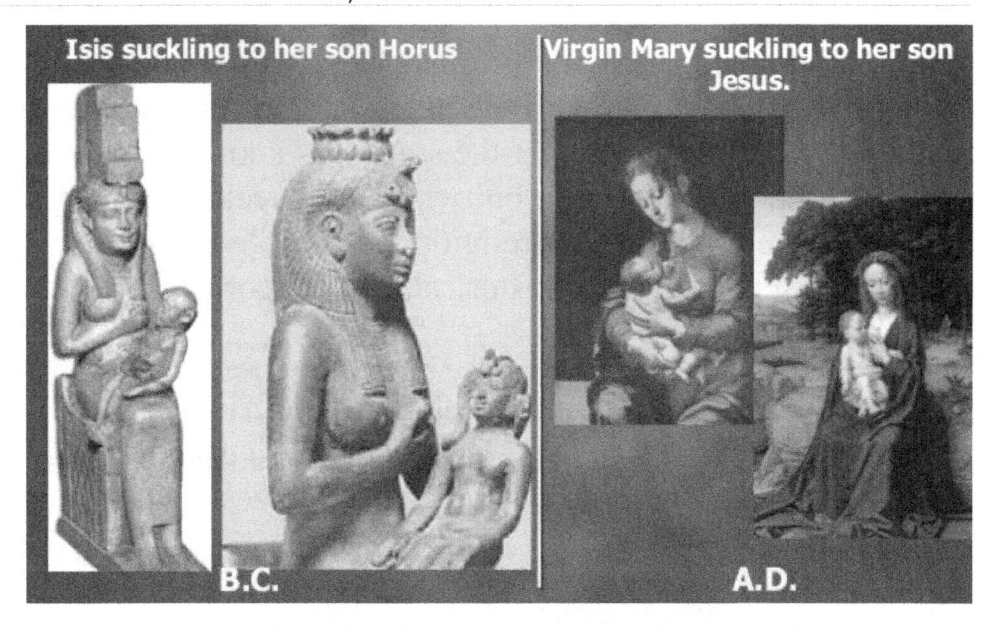

Isis suckling to her son Horus — B.C.

Virgin Mary suckling to her son Jesus. — A.D.

This is a comparison of the original Kemetian concept of the divine mother and child, with the much later adapted version of the allegory. In ancient Kemet the story was a known myth and was not to be taken literally, but when the Greeks and Romans decided to create their new religion they deceived the masses into believing the story was historical, and allegorical.

2. Hor-Sa-Auset, which means Heru, Son of Auset, or Horsieis (Harsiesisin the Greek). This Heru depicted with his forefinger in his mouth which symbolizes the taking in of Right Knowledge.

Hor-Sa-Auset

A Brief Introduction to Kemetian Cosmology, Signs, Symbols, and Rituals
By Faheem Judah-El D.D. D.M.

Hor-Sa-Auset is the original depiction of Jesus the Child

Heru as a child, standing on serpents (crocodiles) and handling scorpions

This is an ancient Kemetian (Egyptian) relief depicting the power of Heru. The writer of Luke 10:19 adapted this concept of Heru and attributed it to Jesus.

Fact: read this Biblical Verse, it was taken out of the knowledge of the Africans of the Nile Valley in ancient Ta-Seti and ancient Kemet.

Luke 10:19
__Behold, I have given you authority to tread on serpents and scorpions, and over all the power of the enemy, and nothing will injure you.__
(Now look at the pictures above, this was a concept in ancient African (Kemetian) spirituality long before any Judeo-Christian concept.)

This is Jesus (Ya'shua) speaking to the 72 disciples that are unnamed but are actually the **Shemsu Heru** or followers of Heru in the original Kemetian teachings.

Luke 10: verse 17: 17 the seventy-two returned with joy and said, "Lord, even the demons submit to us in your name." **(Ask your Pastor to explain to you who were Jesus' 72 unnamed followers)**

In the picture, we see Heru or Heru Pa Khart, Heru the Child treading on Serpents, and handling Scorpions.

*Note: The seventy-two refer to the Students of the Greater Mysteries in the allegory.

This is the original Jesus story from the African Nile Valley, taken by the Greeks, and Romans and converted into the major modern religions of today without your knowledge.

"Behold, I have given you authority to tread on serpents and scorpions, and over all the power of the enemy, and nothing will injure you."

3. The next form of Heru is Heru Behdety, which means Heru who has avenged the death of his father (see the story of Ausar and Set), and flew up to the Orion complex in the form of a winged disk.

This symbol represents the stage in life of working and struggling to develop our higher self, to move up to higher planes of conscious development, so we can vibrate up to our spiritual home.
*Note: Heru Behdety was equivalent to Apollo by the Greeks.

4. The Next form of Heru is Heru-ur, which means Heru the Elder or Heru the Great, known as Harueris to the Greeks. This stage of Heru represents reaching the age of Right Wisdom, the matured self in all senses of the word. In this form Heru is depicted as a hawk-headed male Neter wearing the double crown of Upper and Lower Kemet, the Micro and the Macro, the Subjective and the Objective manifest.

A Brief Introduction to Kemetian Cosmology, Signs, Symbols, and Rituals
By Faheem Judah-El D.D. D.M.

Heru –ur, Heru the Great

5. The last form of Heru is Hor.Akhti, which means Heru on, or of, the Horizon, a form of a new morning sun. He is known as Harmachis by the Greeks. So those are the five forms of Heru which are also the five form of man if our God nature is realized.

Question: you explained Ra-Hor.Akhti before; can you explain what it represents for us?

Answer: Ra.Hor.Akhti represents the combined characteristics of Ra and Heru (Horus of the Horizon). Ra.Hor.Akhti represents the renewed creation process. Ra represents the renewed Heru in the beginning of the first light of day.

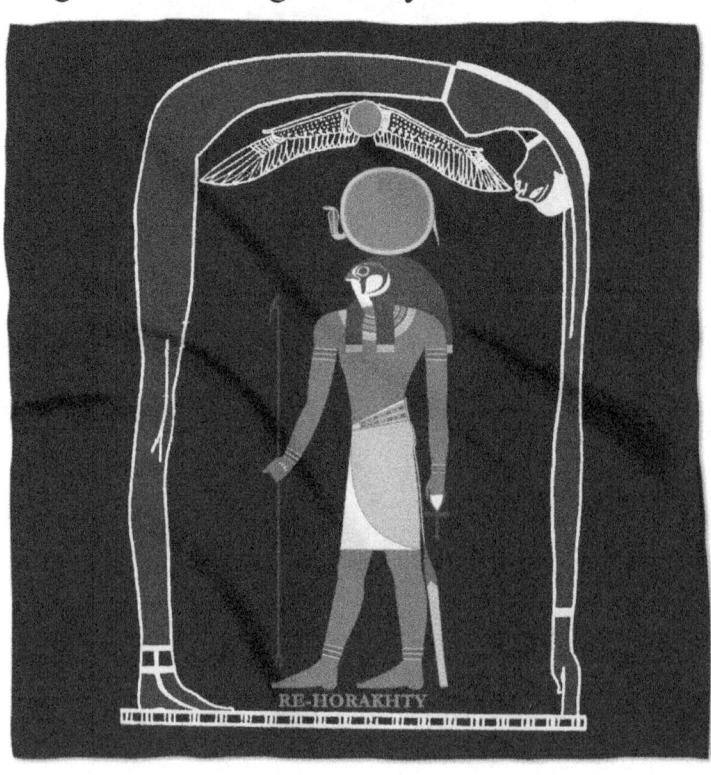

THE COSMIC SIGNS OF HERU

Heru is the Neter of the glorious shining sun. Those born under this sign would risk their lives to avenge their father's death. They courageously face dangers and seldom face catastrophic events.

Strengths: wise, spiritual in nature, brave, pious, observant, optimistic, brilliantly sociable, confident, and motivated to win the best in life, a born leader. They are very family orientated and are welcome rays of light for their beloved.

Weaknesses: In their developmental stage, people under this sign can be unrealistic, stubborn and reluctant to confront problems.

Jobs assumed: Leader in any field, Judge, politicians and media men.

Qualities: Strong-willed and charming.

Negative traits: Stubbornness and inflexibility.

Ideal jobs: Political based roles or Media Promotions, International Relief and Relations, World Affairs.

Planets: The Moon and Sun.

Kemetian animal: The Snake.

Kemetian zodiac compatibility: Heru is compatible with Bastet and Geb

A Brief Introduction to Kemetian Cosmology, Signs, Symbols, and Rituals
By Faheem Judah-El D.D. D.M.

AMEN, AMUN-RA, AMUN, AMON

Kemetian- 8th – 21st January and 1st – 11th February

Attributes: Considerate, observant, strong, determined, and professional

Question: What does Amun Represent?

Answer: *Amun means hidden one,* Amun represents the hidden or underlying power of creation, and the subjective force that animates the universe.

Question: How is Amen defined?

Answer: Amen is hidden and therefore and indefinable, but Amen is the cause, and the universe is the effect. **In spiritual terms Amen is the Spirit of Creation.**

Question: What other Neteru is Amen associated with?

Answer: Amen is associated with Ra (Amen-Ra) (Re), Menu (Min), Ptah, and the Ogdad or City of Eight.

Question: What do Amen and Ra represent when joined together?

Answer: When Amen (The Hidden One), is joined with Ra as Amen-Ra, the two forces combined represent the animated power of creation. Ra is the creative force, and Amen is the hidden force that animates all things, with Amen the all life would be in a state of suspended Animation.

THE COSMIC SIGNS OF AMEN, AMON AMEN-RA

Amon-Ra is the Neter of protection and is considered the king of the Neteru. (The Greeks call Amen Zeus) Amen people are talented and optimistic.

Leadership: Amen people are great leaders and they inspire and encourage others.

Problem Solvers: In any situation, Amon-Ra people are always quick thinkers, confident, and they keep everything calm and under control.

Amon people are happy people, and thanks to their optimism, they very often rub their happiness off on others. They are able to trust their inner voice, and they use it to help others. They are very successful and lucky.

Careers: They can make a career as a consultant, life coach, psychologist, therapist, trainer, or motivational leader, inspiring others to improve their lives. People often come to them for advice. Amon-Ra people make excellent decisions. People born under this sign are intelligent and often become leaders in many walks of life. Amon people are wise, courageous, and diligent.

Character: Secretive

Qualities and Attributes: Powerful, considerate, observant, strong, determined, and professional

Planet: Saturn and the Sun

Kemetian zoo-type (animal): the Ram

Amun-Ra people are compatible with Heru people

Those born under the sign of Anbu – Anubis

9th – 27th May and 29th June – 13th July

Attributes: Great insight, imagination, happy nature, curious, leader and guide

In Ancient Kemetian mythology (Anbu) Anubis is the guardian of the underworld. People born under the sign of Anubis are very passionate and creative. They are very emotional and sensitive; they usually prefer to work alone. Their emotions can be very unpredictable.

Respect: Despite the fact that they are introverts, people born under the sign of Anbu radiate confidence that causes respect from other people.

They freely express their opinion. People of the Anubis sign are very perceptive and conservative. They are very observant and often know in advance about the thoughts and motives of other people.

Careers: Anbu people are interested in professions related to detective work, doctors, nurses, counselor, private investigator, research, education and psychology. They never abandon the goal, even if that goal takes longer to achieve than expected.

Relationships: In relationships, Anbu people are loyal, affectionate and caring. They are happy to take care of their families and homes.

Attributes and Qualities: Truthful and sympathetic to others, adviser, and guide

Character: Controlling and very competitive

Planets: Mercury

Kemetian zoo-type (animal) The Jackal (dog)

Anubis people are compatible with Bastet and Auset people

A Brief Introduction to Kemetian Cosmology, Signs, Symbols, and Rituals
By Faheem Judah-El D.D. D.M.

Those born under the sign of Set

28th May – 18th June and 28th September – 2nd October

Attributes: Free spirit, loving and caring, spontaneous

In Kemetian mythology, Set is known as the Neter of chaos. People born under this Kemetian sign are always looking for change. They can search all life for adventures and thrills. They set themselves high goals and do not stop until they are achieved. These are leaders who do not like to lose or to be in second place. They always solve problems with determination and perseverance. Set's people will not sacrifice their own progress for the sake of everyone else. People of this sign are very sociable and charismatic. They like to be the center of attention. They can become good ministers, motivational speakers or business people (sellers). Set people prefer actions to silence and solitude. They like to move forward all the time. They are always looking for greater information and knowledge. They tend to become leaders in areas that are cutting edge or not very well known by the public.

Attributes: Persistent and determined

Character: Bad Temper

Career: Teacher, Professor, Instructor

Kemetian zoo-type: (animal) Tiger

Set people are compatible with Geb people

Those born under the sign of Bast, Bastet

July 14-28, September 23-27, and October 3-17

In ancient Kemetian mythology Bast (Bastet) is known as the Netert of cats and the Netert of pleasure. She protects women and fertility, as well as love.

Balance and Peace: Bastet always look for balance and peace. They avoid confrontation and stressful situations.

Intuition: Bastet people have very strong intuition and may display some psychic ability. Intuition allows them to see the true motives of people. People born under the sign of Bastet have charming personalities and they love to enjoy life. They surround themselves with pleasant things.

Music and art: Bastet people are inspired by music and art, especially conscious music and art.

Romance: Bastet people are great lovers, affectionate and caring, and they like to be in romantic relationships, they are loyal and devoted partners. They are very emotional and sensitive, but also protect those they love dearly, especially their children. They are affectionate and caring, passionate and they love hard, but if betrayed their counterpart Sekhmet rises up in them which can cause much trouble for the person that betrayed them.

Mystical Nature: People born under the sign of Bastet are mysterious; they are attracted by secrets and sacred knowledge. Their activities may be associated with spiritual science or metaphysics.

Career: Writer, storyteller

Character: Thoughtful and charming, can be possessive, and suspicious

Planets: Sun and the moon

Kemetian zoo-type: (animal) The Cat

Bastet people are compatible with Heru people

Those born under the sign of Sekhmet

29th July – 11th August and 30th October – 7th November

Attributes: Talkative, Silent, observant, moody, happy, sad, responsible, irresponsible, calm, or explosive

In Kemetian mythology, Sekhmet is known as the Netert of war. She is also considered a healer. People born under the Kemetian sign of Sekhmet have a dual identity. On the one hand, they are

disciplined and strict. On the other hand, they are free and like to just go with the flow, without any restrictions.

Perfectionists: They are perfectionists who have a sense of duty and justice. They can become good judges and leaders.

Professional: People born under the sign of Sekhmet are very professional and able to maintain confidentiality. Many people respect them for discipline and favors.

Goals: Their main goal is always to do a perfect job, and keep their pride and integrity. For them, this is just as important as achieving the goal itself.

Powerful: Sekhmet people are best realized in power positions, but they can also thrive as volunteers. They are very optimistic and see the good in things even when faced with obstacles.

Passion: Sekhmet people are very passionate in love, but can be very scornful if betrayed. Sekhmet people can also show their Bastet side of balance and peace, but they also have a side they most people do not want to encounter if they betray a Sekhmet person.

Friendship: A Sekhmet person will be a true friend to the very end, but can also be a worst enemy to the very end.

Those born under the sign of Mut (Moot)
January 22 – 31, September 8 – 22

The Kemetian Netert Mut was the second member of the great Theban triad of divinities, which consisted of her spouse Amen-Rā and her son Khonsu, the Neter of the Moon. She symbolized nature and was regarded as the mother of all things, hence her name *Mut*, "the mother," implies.

Theban Triad: Amen-Ra, Mut, Khonsu

The Netert Mut symbolizes woman and mother. In Kemetian mythology, Mut also symbolizes the divine mother carrying the "solar blood of Ra", her name means **"mother of the world"**. People born under the sign of Mut (Moot) are educators and advocates especially for children. People born under the sign of Mut are usually great mothers and become good parents.

Emotions: Mut people often hide their inner feelings and thoughts, revealing them only to their closest friends and family.

Shyness: Mut people are usually very shy and they only get close to people they are very comfortable with.

Attributes: Knowledgeable, Wise, and Generous

Determined: Mut people are very determined people and know what they want out of life, and they are determined to go after it. Mut people are focused on making their dreams come true, they are charismatic and patient.

Logic: Mut people are rational and logical thinkers, they are excellent debaters. They are loyal friends and companions, sincere with their words and feelings, and seem to have a mysterious nature. Mut people are somewhat conservative, thrifty, and spiritually inclined: they are interested in developing spiritual growth and philosophy.

The Depiction of Mut (Moot): Mut was depicted as a woman with wings, or a vulture wearing the crown of royalty: she was often depicted wearing the down crown of Kemet or the vulture headdress of the "New Kingdom" queens.

Mut (Moot) was the "Giver of Life, The Great Giver of Birth, but not born of any".

The Vulture: During mating, the male Griffon (vulture) spreads his seed in the wind, never physically touching the female, a form of "clean birth" or Immaculate Conception". This is related to the story of the "Immaculate Conception of Heru" after the death of Ausar.

Those born under the sign of Shu

No Kemetian Decan

Greek Influence: January 26 – February 24

The Neter Shu and Tefnut (Tefnoot)

The duality of Shu and Tefnut (Tefnoot) represents the first act of creation, the husband and wife pair represents the expression of duality and polarity.

The Neter Shu

Shu (Su) was the Neter of air and personified the wind and the earth's atmosphere. As the Neter of air, Shu represented the space between the earth and the heavens, and gave the breath of life to all living creatures. Shu was one of the Ennead of Heliopolis, and the first to be created by the self created Neter Atum who created him from his own spittle.

He was the husband and brother of Tefnut (Tefnoot) (moisture), and father of the Nut (Noot) (sky) and Geb (earth). It was thought that his children were infatuated with each other, and remained locked in a perpetual embrace. Shu intervened and held Nut (the sky) above him separating her from his son Geb (the earth). Thus Shu created the atmosphere which allowed life to flourish. Four pillars located at the cardinal points of the world helped Shu maintain the separation of earth and sky, and were known as the "Pillars of Shu".

Shu Characteristics: Creative, talented, warm hearted, great sense of humor, a great story teller, despite your great abilities, you don't always trust yourself and take action because you're afraid you might fail. This can cause you to miss out on many great opportunities.

Career: Counselor, Life Coach, Spiritual Advisor

Your principles guide you in life

Those born under the sign of Geb
February 12 – 29, August 20 – 31

In ancient Kemetian mythology the Neter Geb (Seb) was the Neter of the earth (Ta). He was the father of Ausar, Set, Auset and Nebt-Het.

In ancient Kemet Geb (also known as Seb, or Keb) was one of the Supreme Nine or the Grand Ennead of Heliopolis (City of the Sun). Geb's grandfather was Atum (the self-created one), and his father was the Neter Shu (Neter of air) and his mother was Tefnut (Netert of moisture). Ausar, Auset, Set, and Nebt-Het were the children of Geb and his sister-wife Nut (Netert of the sky). Geb was the third divinity, reigning after his father Shu, and before Ausar. The Nisu Bity was known as the "Heir of Geb".

In the Book Pert-EM-hru: Nsu Bity says "I am decreed to be the Heir, the Lord of the Earth of Geb".

Character: Geb people have kind hearts, and they possess good intuition. They can be overly emotional, charming, and possess magnetism that attracts other people.

Geb people can be very reliable and good friends. They can be very sensitive, but they always remaining cool and tactful. They are diplomatic, and they always think before acting. They can be shy, but if necessary, they can be very persistent. They have a good memory and they never forget what other people have done for them or to them. They are attracted by activities that are useful for the Earth (Ta) and the environment. Professions related to teaching, counseling or literature will suit them.

☥

A Brief Introduction to Kemetian Cosmology, Signs, Symbols, and Rituals
By Faheem Judah-El D.D. D.M.

Those born under the sign of Het Heru

Date Used After Greek Influence: May 26 – June 24

The Netert Het-Heru

Het Heru People are passionate, talented musicians and dancers, and highly emotional. Het Heru people are very charming people, but their highly emotional nature can show their jealousy and anger.

Het Heru people are romantic and great lovers; they enjoy walks on the beach, romantic dinners, intimate and private time with their lovers.

Het Heru people are extroverts; they love a good party or social gathering of any kind.

Careers: Public speaker, minister, activist, motivational speaker, any service related field, arts and entertainment.

Het Heru - Hathor was one of the most important divinities in Ancient Kemet. She held many titles and had many attributes, functions and duties to perform in the Ancient Kemetian pantheon.

Het Heru was the sister of Aset, and assisted her in locating the parts of her husband Ausar's body parts that were cut up into 14 pieces and thrown in the Nile River by his disagreeable brother Set. Het Heru was the Netert of music, love, and birth and nourishment. Het Heru is associated with harmonics.

Symbol: Sistrum - vibrations, rhythms 'and tones

Hathor was one of the most ancient Kemetian divinities, but was highly recognized by the early Greeks students after they occupied ancient Kemet. Het Heru was associated with Aphrodite by the Greeks.

A Brief Introduction to Kemetian Cosmology, Signs, Symbols, and Rituals
By Faheem Judah-El D.D. D.M.

Traditional Dates Based on the Decans: March 11-31, October 18-29, and December 19-31

Date Used After Greek Influence: February 25 – March 26

Auset – Isis

Picture courtesy of Emhotep Richards

Auset, Aset – Meri-Auset which means Beloved Auset

Characteristics of the Kemetian Zodiac Sign of Auset: If your sign is Auset, you are a person who is direct and tells the truth. You are full of positive energy and love to be creative, and explore new things; you are full of confidence, a great lover, and a great lover of life. Those born under the sign of Auset are compassionate, and have great nurturing instincts.

Auset people like balance and order, they don't like too much needless pressure, they have inner wisdom and strength, and they use logic and intuition to see things from a higher perspective. They don't take things too seriously, and they have a great sense of humor.

Auset people care for those around them, they have a great sense of community leadership, and they are no non-sense people who will discipline those as needed. They also look for the best in all people, and they live by high spiritual standards.

About the Netert Auset: She was known in the African Nile Valley as Auset, and later known by the Greeks as Isis.

Auset represented the ideal mother and wife. She was the patron Netert of love, joy, nurturing, and nature. She protected the dead, children, the poor, and sinners. The City of Paris France (Par-Isis) was named after Isis –Auset.

The name Auset means throne and she is often shown wearing a throne on her head. The Nisu (Pharoah) was viewed as her child, and he sat on the throne she provided.

Auset was the wife and brother of Ausar (Osiris), and the mother of Heru (Horus). When Set murdered Ausar (Osiris), Auset (Isis) helped resurrect him. She gathered Ausar's body parts from along the Nile Valley and with the help of the Neter Tehuti restored life to his body. This death and resurrection was deeply ingrained in Ancient Kemetian culture. They believed the Nile flooded every year from the tears that Auset cried for Ausar-Osiris.

Ausar and Auset

The pre-creative state of the world and cosmology

Questions and Answers

Question: Can you explain the Egyptian concept of Cosmology

Answer: The ancient world cosmological concept consisted of polarity: Yin/yang, hot/cold, light/darkness, dryness/moisture, but the ancient Kemetians were fascinated with the polarities of light and darkness. Ancient Kemetian Cosmology was Natural Cosmology, as taught by Heliopolitan Cosmologists in ancient Kemet. These teachings date back to the old Kingdom around (2700BC), it starts with the primordial ocean known as "Nun". Nun was boundless, chaotic, and formless in all directions, was nothingness or unorganized chaos.

Out of the chaotic waters of Nun came the Sun Neter Ra (Khepe-Ra – Atum – Ra), Ra came into being out of its own self.

9 And Elohim said: 'Let the waters under the heaven (Nut) be gathered together unto one place, and let the dry land (Geb/Earth) appear.' And it was so.

HOLY QURAN

SURAH (CHAPTER 96) Bismillah Al-Rahman Al Raheem

96:1 READ! IN THE NAME OF THY LORD, AND CHERISHER, WHO CREATED –

96:2 CREATED MAN OUT OF A MERE CLOT OF CONGEALED BLOOD (A-DAM = BLOOD)

96:3 PROCLAIM, AND THY LORD IS MOST BOUNTYFUL,

96:4 HE (HUWA) WHO TAUGHT THE USE OF THE PEN (TEHUTI)

96:5 TAUGHT MAN THAT WHICH HE KNEW NOT.

SYMBOL OF ISLAM – SUN/MOON MYSTERIES

This section of Genesis tells us that Maat is the foundation of the world; this is why Maat's symbol is a stone platform or foundation, representing the stable base of the universe on which all order is built. Ma-at or Ma'yet represents the principle of cosmic order the concept by which the universe is governed. Maat signifies balance, harmony, order, and peace between all the cosmic forces of nature.

Maat is maintained in the world by the correct actions of man, and the highest objective of the earthly man is to rise up the spirit man within, or to develop the higher consciousness to perfection.

EVERLASTING LIFE

THE SYMBOL PHYSICAL OF LIFE

BIRTH, MALE AND FEMALE PRINCIPLES, SPIRIT AND PHYSICAL, MICRO AND MACRO,

INFINITE AND FINITE

MORTAL AND IMMORTAL

THE KEMETIAN STORY OF CREATION

The Kemetian Creation Epic adapted by Faheem Judah-El D.D. with explanation by Faheem Judah-El D.D.

In the (bara) (barashit) beginning, there was only the *Nun* (Nun/Nu/Ny): the great celestial waters of the Unmanifest (spirit-micro); the depths of the nighttime sky. *(Nun represents the unpolarized state of matter.) In the human being, Nun represents the state of unconsciousness, like during sleep. All of our mental powers are there, but they are in a chaotic state. Nun represents each person's potential, which needs to be reorganized, sorted out, and utilized.*

Swimming within this primordial Deep was the mighty Ogdoad: The eight Neteru. In the Kemetian Creation Text it tells us, before the (bara) beginning of all things, there was a liquidy primeval abyss everywhere, it was endless, and without boundaries or conformity. We call this cosmic ocean "the chaotic waters", NUN.

Modern science is in agreement with the Kemetian description of the origin of the universe as being a great abyss. This great abyss is a cosmic place where there are neither electrons nor protons, only neutrons forming one big dense nucleus. The Bible says:

2. Now the earth was unformed and void, and darkness was upon the face of the deep; and the spirit of Elohim hovered over the face of the waters.

The Ogdad (The Four Pairs)

The Ancient Kemetian text tells us that Nun (the pre-creation chaos, place of all potential) possessed characteristics that were identified with four pairs of primordial forces. Each pair represents the primeval dual-gendered twins.

Their names are Nun and Nunet, deities of the watery abyss; Heh and Hehet, deities of infinite space; Kek and Keket, deities of darkness; and Amon and Amonet, deities of the invisible.

NAME	REPRESENTATION	SYMBOLISM
NUN – NAUNET (FROGS + SNAKES)		**PRIMEVAL WATERS**
HEH – HEHET (FROGS + SNAKES)		**INFINITY OF SPACE**
KEK – KEKET (FROGS + SNAKES)		**DARKNESS**
AMEN – AMENET (FROGS + SNAKES)		**INVISIBILITY**

The Four Males: NUN, HEH, KEK, AMEN

The Four Females: NAUNET, HEHET, KEKET, AMENET

The four males of the pairs are represented as frogs. The four females of the pairs are represented as serpents. These pairs were symbolic for "The Masculine / feminine aspects or duality. The four pairs are equivalent to the four forces of the universe.

THE STRONG NUCLEAR FORCE – MALE – HU

THE WEAK NUCLEAR FORCE – FEMALE – HEEA

GRAVITY

ELECTRO-MAGNETISM

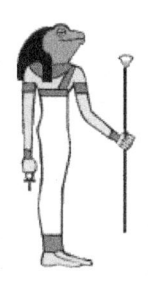

KEK = SYMBOL OF DARKNESS

"These are the eight pre-creation forces" the number 8 represents "potential" a new beginning."

The (Ogdad) is 4 Males x 4 Females = 8, then comes creation which is 9. (The Supreme Nine –The Grand Ennead)

THE OGDAD

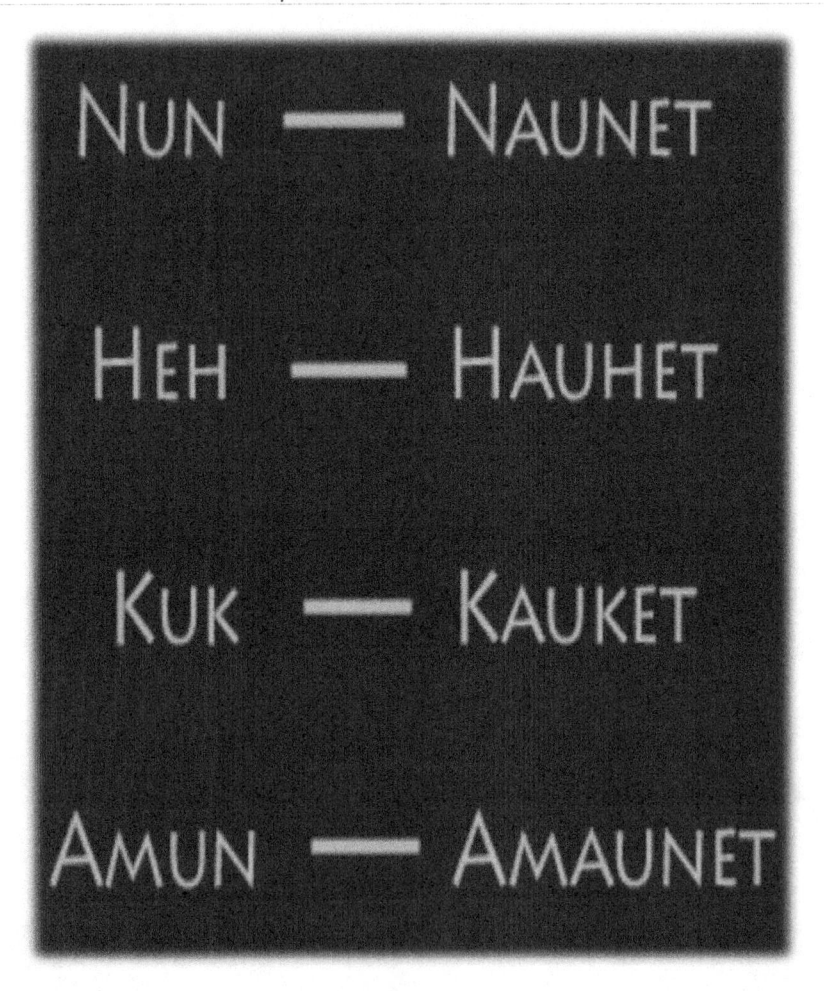

A Brief Introduction to Kemetian Cosmology, Signs, Symbols, and Rituals
By Faheem Judah-El D.D. D.M.

```
NUN     —     NAUNET

HEH     —     HAUHET

KUK     —     KAUKET

AMUN    —     AMAUNET
```

In the symbolism of the Ogdad, in the eight manifest worlds these beings are depicted with their legs tied together which implies their nature is "action", but while in the subjective realm (before creation) they are inert. (Not active) Having their legs tied in the subjective realm points to their potential energies.

WHY THE SNAKE? Because the snake is a metaphor for the spiral of life, look at a baby's hair pattern when he/she is born, the baby spirals down into creation from the universe and the mother. The serpent represent "The Netert or Goddess" on the walls of ancient Kemet. It is the female aspect that represents the active potent power in the universe.

WHY THE FROG? Because frogs are symbols of the change in a season, frogs are seen in great numbers just before the yearly flooding of the Nile river, the frog is seen as evolving, from a tadpole to a frog, (from water to land) the frog represents **"new life"**. Just as a baby goes from the water in the sack of the mother to breathing air as it enters new life in this world.

These primordial deities swam within the waters on Nun, guarding the Great Egg that incubated the Creator.

In time, the egg began to hatch. It split into two halves, dividing the waters of the *Nun* into the upper and lower levels, and making between them a space wherein the Creator could fashion the world.

From the egg arose a single blue Lotus. It raised high above the darkness of the abyss, and opened its great petals. Within its golden heart rested a beautiful young Netjer, the **Creator Amen-Re**, with one single finger pressed against His lips in Silence.

Light streamed from the body of this Divine Child, banishing darkness to the far reaches of the universe. Like a phoenix with flaming plumage, He arose, uttering a cry that shattered the eternal silence.

This was the first sound- the first Word - and that Word manifested as a living Netjer, Tehuti was His name: the Self-Created, the Logos, Wisdom, The eternal Son who is One with The Father.

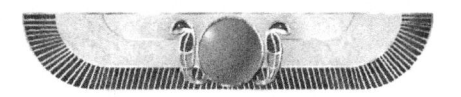

Beginning

NOTES

A Brief Introduction to Kemetian Cosmology, Signs, Symbols, and Rituals
By Faheem Judah-El D.D. D.M.

A Brief Introduction to Kemetian Cosmology, Signs, Symbols, and Rituals
By Faheem Judah-El D.D. D.M.